Graceful Reflections of Transition

Lessons from the Dying

Myra L. Lovvorn

"Sylvia call 911…"

Why dad?

"Its your mom."

I ran upstairs to see my mom's chest caving in with each heart beat.

I call 911…. "….. does she have a pulse." . . . not sure.. her body is constricting with each heart beat…

"Do you know CPR…" I hesitated, as i did know it .. but looking at my mom i knew it was not going to help her… so i put the phone down and held my Mother.

I talked to her… told her it was ok for her to do what she needed to do. Told her that i would be alright and that I would take care of dad.

I felt her relax a little … saw the tension on her face calm itself.

I removed her glasses while telling her she wouldn't be needing these anymore…

and I added "not that you can see out of em anyways mom

… geez they are filthy!"

And her heartbeats were slowing.. the violence of the caving in was getting calmer… and everything stopped. And i quit hearing.

I quit feeling her physically…

Somehow my spirit got wrapped up in hers …. and we began to move.

Like on a railway thru a tunnel. And there was noise that I couldn't distinguish.

And I was holding my mother tightly … supporting her now limp body.

And I could not understand what was happening.. yet I knew she was passing… and there wasn't any fear.

There was no screaming .. no crying .. no sadness … nothing accept that light.

Somewhere ahead there was a huge light … tho I could not see the source.

And all the noise stopped.

All the motion stopped.

And the cart or buggy we were riding in started going backwards… picking up speed.

And I realized … my mom was not sitting beside me …

And I knew she was gone…

and that I was not.

Sylvia DeVoss, 2002

Introduction & Thanks

Thanks to Divine Love - we do not know what will happen in the future. Looking back, we can see many mysteries and lessons after we are over the shock of a death. How could we cope with the present if we knew a death was going to occur on a given day, or worse yet, a birthday or holiday?

The following book is intended to share some of the stories from my life and work as a hospice nurse, interactions with family and friends, and in my personal life as well. Please accept that the names of many of the dying have been changed to honor their journey. The stories are from my memory, my perspective and in no way is perfectly how they occurred.

Sylvia DeVoss is and artist and a dear friend who shared her story and much of the artwork in this book. Her experience with her mother in this opening segment was a blessing that she was allowed to journey with her mother to the light and then realized that she had returned to continue her own life.

Thank you, Sylvia for your friendship, sharing your talent and your amazing journey in this life.

A special thanks to Johanna Giraldo for suggesting creating this book. Her support in transcribing this book from stories I told her and supporting me to write these stories added so much to what you are going to experience.

To Diane Cree Kane who was my partner through many of these stories as the hospice social worker and confidant when sometimes the 'going got rough'. We continue to support one another on this journey, though now through presencing with dying friends and family. Loving you!!

Why this book?

In 2015, a friend (boss and colleague), Brenda Clarkson and I wrote a book about the Heart of Hospice: Core Competencies for Reclaiming the Mystery, hoping that we could encourage hospice workers to look at their practice and learn from their experiences. It was well received by a few hospices, however with the current regulatory climate in health care, money became the driving force and not the spiritual development of hospice staff. Brenda and I with our colleagues learned how to do end-of-life care 'by the seat of our pants' and we wanted to share some of our wisdom with others.

The shell became the framework for our book with twelve 'core competencies' that were spiritually focused. When this book became 'real', this framework was perfect to organize some of the stories from my experience of the dying. I realized talking with Johanna Giraldo that I had so many wonderful stories and we needed to publish them. Then, Sylvia DeVoss had stories to tell and amazing artwork to share as well. Our desire is to combine the art with the artful dying experiences to normalize the process. Please accept this book in the Love and Spirit that it was gifted to me through the many beautiful families and experiences in transition.

Well . . . Away we go!!

In the Beginning . . .

My first death happened in 1978 while working summers during nursing school. She was in her 40's, one of my favorite patients, and had ovarian cancer. I was assigned to provide 'activities of daily living' care (ADL's) and when I finished my assignments we spent time sitting in her room and talking. This was back in the day we had enough staff so we had time to spend with our patients. There were many lessons for a new 'nurse' working with 'my friend'.

As I left on Wednesday evening, I turned to tell her "See you tomorrow". She smiled and said "I hope so". I came in to work the next day and went by her room only to see the bed freshly made. This means one of two things; either she was in the intensive care unit (ICU) or she went home. This particular day, I learned that patients could go to two different 'homes'. Sometimes 'going home' meant to the spirit world, or wherever they believed they would go. As I reflect today on that patient encounter, I realize that when she said "I hope so" she was telling me we would not see each other again in this physical lifetime. As always, reflection on our experience tells us the lessons we could learn, if we pay attention.

Some of the hardest lessons are learned when our loved ones die. As a new nurse for 5 years, my mother developed a condition that would eventually end her life. She was diagnosed with a fungal infection requiring daily infusions of a very toxic anti-fungal medication, that the health care team in the hospital felt I could give her each day at home, after I finished my night shift working in the hospital. This meant I worked from 10:30PM, for 7 days straight and get off at 7 AM each day, then go to her home, access her IV in her arm and wait a hour while the medication infused. On my last night shift that week, my father called me at work at 6:00 AM to tell me something was wrong! I left work early only to find that Mother was unconscious and bleeding from her mouth. Whoa . . .!!

We loaded her in the car, remember this was November, 1986 and emergency services were not as efficient as they are today. My father went to work, as usual, and my roommate and I took her to the hospital where they had started her treatment. (This is another story that could be considered "not the best practice").

She was in the emergency room (ER) all day and at 1:30 PM we decided to go shopping for Christmas presents, since we had been up for almost 20 hours. When we came into the hospital, we passed the nurses from the ER taking Mother to the ICU, in a hurry! This was when hospitals had very strict visiting hours so I could not see her until the 4:00 visiting time (for only 10 minutes).

When we entered the room, it was obvious she was not doing well. We were told that she was still bleeding because the anti-fungal had destroyed her platelets and she could not clot. They were giving her platelets hoping this would help her clot normally, however I felt this would not work. We had to leave and were allowed to visit again at 6:00 PM.

At exactly 6:00 PM when we entered the room, she was unconscious, unresponsive and it was obvious to me that she was not going to live long. I had no idea how I knew this at the time, however now I realize this was a gift that I would utilize in my work with the dying for over 25 years.

My roommate at the time was a registered nurse who worked with me on the night shift and had been with me through the entire process. We both worked in the ICU and were very knowledgeable about monitors and heart rhythms and while standing at the foot of my Mother's bed, heart stopped!! I looked at my friend who affirmed and encouraged me just by her look.

As we watched the monitor, I knew since Mother was in the ICU so the staff would be coming soon to do cardiopulmonary resuscitation (CPR) since she had no documentation to let her die (Do Not Resuscitate orders or DNR's were rare). My father worked until 5:30 PM and would be there about 6:15 or 6:30. As I was pondering all this, we realized that her pacemaker had started her heart beating again and this could 'buy us some time' until Daddy could get there.

As expected, the staff burst into the door to start CPR and I just lay across my Mother refusing to let them do anything with her. Believe me, they were not happy and after much insistence, they left the room since her pacemaker was now working and no need to do CPR. After a few minutes the cardiologist came to the door and said we had to leave because they wanted to do an EKG to see what was going on with her heart. I refused to leave, giving him a complete report of exactly what had happened, "her heart stopped and her pacer had captured her ventricle at a rate of 70 BPM, and she was dying"! I knew that the pacer was keeping her heart beating until my Father could get to the hospital to sign the paper for her to be considered a do not resuscitate (DNR). The cardiologist was not happy, and we refused to leave her bed after the 6PM visiting time was over. As I said before, this was 1986 just as the Hospice movement was just getting started.

Well, I am quite sure you have guessed the rest . . . Mother took her last breath at 8:30 PM with her loving family around her bed in the ICU. This was quite an experience for us as well as the staff. One nurse asked me after she died, "how did you know?"

This is something I have asked myself on numerous occasions while doing this work for the past 40-plus years,. I am convinced now that it was by 'GRACE' that I was able to hear my intuition and could let her die. That is one of the questions I have for GOD when I transition.

"How did I know"?!!

"How DO I Know??"

Sustaining the Self

I was a novice (a novice in hospice is when you are just beginning on this end-of-life care path) when a colleague and I decided to attend a funeral for her client who was not one of my patients and was not someone I knew.

We sat respectfully at the back of the church during the service, and about three-fourths of the way through the service, I began to cry uncontrollably. It was not something anybody said. I just could not stop crying. It was so much that I had to leave the service.

This was very disturbing for me and for my colleagues since I did not have any emotional attachment with the family or the deceased. I knew my reaction was out of character and there was something else I had to take care of. Being new to hospice, I felt lost and I knew I had to talk to someone who was familiar with death and dying.

When it was safe to drive, I went to the office to meet with our chaplain in hopes of understanding why this happened. After being consoled, he asked me how I was taking care of my 'little' self and I realized at that moment that I was not and had not been taking care of ME.

Wanting to be successful, compassionate and 'the best caregiver' I could be, I was overextending and taking things personally. The chaplain pointed out that my grief and tears was not for the person who died, however was for all the souls that I had been present with up until that moment and had not grieved for them. These included my mother, other family and friends as well as patients in my nursing career and my hospice patients.

I now realize that these feelings pile up and something suddenly triggers them and I experienced a great emotional release. I remembered my mother's death, my grandmother's death, my favorite aunt's death. This release was about all the death I had not dealt with up until that point in my life.

That day I understood the importance of taking care of yourself. The ability to understand that talking with someone about the feelings we have is very important to becoming the 'Big Self' when giving so much to the dying. I have since learned that the 'giving' does not come from me. It comes THROUGH me from Source.

Moving Through Fear

Being on-call for the dying can be fear-laden at times, out at night, driving alone trying to find someone's home who is dying and suffering, or in need of something you cannot provide.

Early in my end-of-life career with Hospice on call, we answered phone calls directly from the client, and often from a 'dead sleep'. On one weeknight around 1:30 AM, I received a call from a gentleman in a panic. He was around 55 years old, and was dying from stomach cancer. He lived alone and was 'throwing up' and could not stop. Not knowing this gentleman, my anxiety was very high, fearful that I would not know what to do.

As usual it takes 30-50 minutes to get to a home after receiving a call. He let me in and in fact, he had intractable vomiting. There are many more details here that I will spare the reader, as many may not be medical professionals. At the time, the emergency kits that are standard today from hospice agencies were not available so the only medications he had were not helpful. We tried all the calming things we knew and after 45 minutes with no relief I called the physician on call.

He was sleeping as well and ordered medication to stop his nausea. Luckily, we had a local pharmacy who did on-call visits and the owner of the pharmacy went to the office, retrieved the medication and delivered it as quickly as he could. After another 45-60 minutes, still no relief so I called the physician on call again and eventually he heard the fear in my voice and we called for an ambulance to take this dying patient to the hospital. It took 30 minutes for them to arrive and the suffering was almost overwhelming for both of us.

This was a very difficult experience for me because I was very afraid and did not know what to do. In fact there was nothing I could do to relieve his suffering and that moment.

By reflecting on this episode, talking with our counselor and other colleagues, I understood that this was this gentleman's path to dying. My role was to be with him providing as much comfort as was possible. He was going to suffer, however with me there he was comforted knowing he was not alone. This was very supportive as I moved through my own feelings of ear and continued my role with the dying.

Connecting

Mr. Demaskus had lung cancer and was in the hospital. He was deeply religious, very devout and had occupied a very high position in his local church. Our team visited him in the hospital to fulfill his wish to go home to die. He was on oxygen and was very sick when we met him, sometimes was confused. His wife was his caregiver and was in agreement.

When he arrived home, the confusion worsened and he started to try to climb out of bed, didn't want to wear his oxygen mask, and became a little belligerent with his wife. Our team divided our visits so we could go very often to help the wife manage his behavior. He finally got weak enough that he could not get out of bed anymore.

Three days before he died, he started reaching out over the guardrail on the bed, and would sometimes say "I can't get there, I can't get there, just six more feet, just six more feet" over and over. At other times, he would say things that seemed a little incoherent as though talking to the unseen.

It became clear he was transitioning to the other side, however there appeared to be a 'gap' that was six feet out of his reach. His wife tried to find out how to support him when we realized the disconnection might be on the other side that it is not time yet. She accepted this and just sat with him. She called us in the morning of the fourth day to report he had transitioned during the night and that he had finally 'connected' with the place and he was smiling when he died.

Centering

My daily spiritual practice included connecting with a quiet place inside each day creating a 'center' inside that is available as a touchstone when faced with emotional or difficult situations. The following event proved the importance of centering to be able to cope in a difficult situation.

Benny was a 38 year-old man who was a very successful gamer. I say that however the story lacks intensity unless you could see his bedroom. He had a modest home however, in his bedroom, he had several (more than 3) 50-inch plus TV screens connected to controls and speakers for a virtual experience in gaming and Benny was dying from colon cancer. His family was very supportive and the entire team became involved in his care. Of note, Benny desired to remain in his bedroom, in his recliner and rarely slept in his bed.

As he declined, he continued to 'game' with his friends around the world. He was the Gold Standard for a person directing their care and our team was open to his way of dying. Benny refused medications and most of the usual supporting durable medical equipment (like the electric bed and other traditional equipment). His primary nurse spent time listening to Benny to determine what his goals were and sometimes this was difficult because he was a very quiet, introverted person.

In the end, Benny agreed to a pain pump that gave him medication to relieve his pain so he could remain in his room enjoying gaming as long as he was able. The day he died, his family called and I was the nurse to respond. As I entered the home, his family was present from out of town and his employer with other co-workers were present as well. We shared info regarding how he died and who found him, though I was not given the details.

Much to my surprise, as I entered his bedroom, Benny was in his recliner, slumped over, propped up on his elbows with his head hanging down. He had lost most of his muscle mass as well as all fat tissue and was very thin. As the nurse who attends a death, I was the one who would verify that he was dead. We call that 'pronouncing'. To be able to pronounce Benny dead, I had to listen to his chest with my stethoscope for at least one minute while feeling for a pulse in his arm.

As I knelt down to assess Benny for breathing and his heart rate, I suddenly realized his eyes were hanging out of their sockets, dangling from the nerves because of the loss of fat tissue. At that moment I had to stop because it was all I could do not to react. I decided to connect with my inner guide, get centered and breathe. As I centered, I was able to begin my assessment, listening to his chest and as suspected he had no pulse or heart rate. The bluish color in his face was also a clear indication that he was dead. However, it took me a little longer than a minute to regroup, and I used the stethoscope as an excuse to stay kneeling until I could compose my nonverbal expression to be able to stand up and face his family. By trying to appear normal to his family, they felt this was normal because an outburst for emotion or disdain from me might have compounded their grief. They were gracious. His boss and co-workers assisted with his body removal and others provided support for the younger family members. In the end, this experience was best for all of us. Including me.

I was able to realize how important my daily practice of centering, breath work and energy clearing had become for my professional practice, and not just my personal life.

Comforting

'Want to make God laugh? Tell Her your plan'! Some days I thought I knew how a home visit would 'roll out'. I learned quickly that my plan might need to be changed.

On a joint visit with the social worker we received a phone call to see a new patient. We drove to the country to meet with the family and to give them information to sign and start hospice care. We usually order equipment and get medicine, whatever they need on the first visit.

Traditionally, hospice was developed to provide six months of care, supporting the dying person and their family through death and then the counseling staff continues to follow the bereaved family for twelve months after the death. Well not this time.

We were told that the patient had been diagnosed with extensive cancer and had come home the day before from a long, protracted hospital stay.

We were met at the door by Mrs. Carson's daughter, about 35 years of age and was extremely distraught, unable to talk and begged us to help her mother.

She ran back into her mother's room and we quickly followed while through 'telepathic communication' the social worker and I understood Mrs Carson was dying. The social worker led the daughter into another part of the house while I prepared Mrs. Carson to transition peacefully.

When I went into her room, I noticed the head of the bed was all the way up, she had a mask on, and was gasping for air. I discovered Mrs. Carson was taking her last 'gasps' of air called 'agonal breathing'.

What I found was the oxygen face mask was connected to a 'suction machine' that was removing any oxygen that Mrs. Carson could get and might be adding to her discomfort, however was not causing her to die sooner. She was unresponsive, dying from her condition, which indicated her spirit had 'already left' and her body was completing the dying process.

I removed all the mechanical equipment from around the immediate bedside, cleaned her up and positioned her with the cover under her arms and the head of the bed up enough that she was able to have a more relaxed breathing effort. She did not need any supplemental oxygen and to my pleasant surprise, she began a less labored breathing pattern, as though she wanted to wait until her daughter could come back in the room.

'Grace' filled the room and I did not need to do anything. As soon as I had the thought, the social worker brought the daughter into the room at the exact right moment to see her mother. She was so relieved to see that her mother was calm, and no longer struggling, though we knew she was dying. As with most Grace-filled experiences, we have no idea how long it was before Mrs. Carson stopped breathing, however it was perfect. Her daughter was able to be with her while the social worker called family and I was able to talk with the physician, call the chaplain and had the paperwork signed so we could pronounce Mrs. Carson at home.

Though Mrs. Carson was only in hospice for 45 minutes, bereavement counselors supported the daughter for the 12 months after the death. By being open to the change in plans, we were able to comfort the daughter, allow her to experience a Graceful death process with her mother.

Crusaders of birth
Created Earth
Filled my lungs with ecstasy
Blew life inside of me

Thoughts coming near and far
Rays bouncing star to star
Guardian Angels please..
Never
Never
Let go of me

Collaborating

Collaboration occurs on many levels when complex death experiences occur, for example when caring for Mr. Clark, who was in his mid-fifties and diagnosed with amyotrophic lateral sclerosis (ALS). He was wheelchair bound, could barely move enough to manipulate his wheelchair. Everything else was paralyzed. He had a tube in his trachea to breathe, which made it very hard for him to communicate. He had a little ventilator that hooked to his tracheotomy tube (trache tube), because he was not able to breathe on his own and he depended on this machine to breathe. The medical team suggested putting in a feeding (PEG) tube in his belly to feed him artificially and he said he did not want it.

His wife cared for him and his two teenage children were often involved in his care. He was able to communicate with his wife through a computer program and she agreed it was too hard and he was never going to get better than he was right then. They had a big family meeting and decided that he was going to have the ventilator removed, and he was just going to die. He had decided that he did not want to "keep going on like this". He was done! They on the day to remove the ventilator - on his birthday and his family would all be present.

We had huge discussions in our hospice office about it because it's a big decision for someone to decide they just want to die. We take care of people dying all the time but, when they decide when they are going to die, that is a whole other story. The date they chose was on a weekend which is on-call for us.

We had one particular nurse, Ms. S., who was very religious and was adamant that this was wrong, that this meant 'killing him'. Our doctor at the time, who was brilliant, told this nurse this was something she really had to look at because this was not her issue, it had nothing to do with her. This was Mr. Clark's decision, and we as an organization had to honor his decision. He was in our care and we just had to support him. The staff had much discussion with social work and the chaplain. Everyone was involved. So, our doctor was going to go with Mr. Clark's primary hospice nurse. The weekend staff would be available if needed. The day came and the nurse who was supposed to go was sick, and the doctor who was supposed to go could not go. Somebody had to go!

Guess who was on call? Ms. S. and the doctor who had to attend now was his primary doctor, the doctor from the clinic who was not a hospice physician, where he used to go to all the time. The stories MS. S. told later were absolutely profound about the love that was there; the feeling that was there. They gave him medication so he would not feel anxiety about not being able to breathe, however just enough so he could be a little bit awake, but not really. The wife knew when he was ready and she actually took the ventilator off. He died peacefully within two minutes.

Ms. S. was in tears telling the story in out hospice meeting, about how beautiful it was, how wonderful it was, how loving the family was. She made a complete shift and the thing that was the most profound was this doctor takes care of ALS patients all the time and he had never seen someone die. He had never witnessed someone die. It totally changed his practice.

The compassion that was shared with Mr. Clark's family and that patient was miraculous. It was quite divine that these two groups of people ended up being together for his death.

Building Strengths

Mr. Boyd was in the surgical intensive care unit (SICU) following two months of surgical interventions with no resolution. He knew he was dying, and he wanted to go home to share his final days with his family. The staff in the intensive care unit believed his care was too complex to be delivered at home, especially as most of the care tasks would be delegated to family members.

The end-of-life mystery watcher team of professionals explored all options with Mr. Boyd and his family, who were scared however confident that by pulling together and utilizing home hospice they could fulfill his last wish. Part of the mystery watchers' task was to collaborate with the unit staff to help them to see the family's strengths as a valuable resource with which to meet Mr. Boyd's needs. Once the hospital staff were on board with Mr. Boyd's desire to go home, they taught the family members and end-of-life caregivers alike all the intricacies of his care and made the necessary arrangements for a smooth transition home.

His family took great pride learning all the 'tricks of the trade' that they needed, and although they were individually a little apprehensive, collectively they felt confident about their ability to follow the end-of-life plan of care. In fact, they said they had never felt stronger than when working together to make sure Mr. Boyd's dying wish was granted.

Mr. Boyd died comfortably two days after returning home, surrounded by his family. His wish was fulfilled!

Guiding Good-byes

When caring for young dying persons, the team will draw on many experiences to support the family and the caregivers. Ms. Simpson was in her late 40's with colon cancer that was resistant to many rounds of treatment, surgeries, chemo and radiation leaving her weak and with many care needs. She was a very well-known artist living with a partner who was devoted to her, however with very little skills in the area of physical care and fearful of death. With the support of the caregiver aids in our organization as well as the nursing staff, her partner became more and more comfortable with the personal care.

However, Ms. Simpson's partner was emotionally and spiritually 'lost' in dealing with the possibility of death. This is where the social work and chaplain staff were able to support her through the feelings she had and over time assist her to reach a level of trust. The staff met often to discuss this family as the culture was not accepting of same-gender couples who lived a quiet life that was at risk of being exposed. Over time, both Ms. Simpson and her partner felt accepted and were able to feel their grief and deal with it in a constructive manner.

During our Tuesday morning interdisciplinary meeting (started around 8:00 AM), I was called out of the meeting to a phone call from Ms. Simpson's partner. Her voice was very calm, almost euphoric, which was unusual. She wanted to let me know that Ms. Simpson had died about 4:30 AM and she had decided not to call our team to wake us up and just stayed with Ms. Simpson until our office opened.

Our team had been able to 'guide' this good-bye , allowing time for a healthy grieving experience for her partner.

Honoring Truth

Amyotrophic lateral sclerosis (ALS) is one of the most difficult end-of-life conditions the mystery watcher caregiver might face. As a nurse with the veteran's administration (VA), I visited Robert, who was a Gulf-War veteran and had developed symptoms of ALS in the previous year of our meeting. He lived with two 'house-mates' who loved to play video games and competed internationally. When Robert became less active due to his neurological condition, his friends moved his bedroom into the den closer to the gaming center and began adapting the controls so he could continue to participate.

When I first visited, we discussed what his goal was for his end-of-life care. This is a difficult decision and I found that quite often, no one discusses this with the ALS population. As the disease progresses, they become completely dependent on EVERYTHING. Feeding, daily hygiene, and eventually breathing. Robert was very clear that he was not interested in having a breathing machine, or a PEG tube and when he could no longer breathe, he would be ready to die.

He had this documented in writing for his house mates to follow and we communicated this with his physicians and care team at the VA. Over a month or so, Robert was able to enjoy his gaming at shorter and shorter periods, sleeping more and more and finally he stopped eating due to the 'fear' of choking.

At this time, the care team from the VA visited to support the housemates in the grief process and assisted with the financial arrangements of his home after his death. With the coordination of a local hospice agency, the necessary medications and support for a comfortable death were in place.

Robert became less and less responsive and after a couple of days, died comfortably with his housemates present. Robert was very young. However, he was in control of his death just as he controlled his life. By being open to his wishes and desires, he was able to settle his 'estate', direct his care and honor his truth at the end of his life.

Transforming Knowledge

I was called to Mrs. Johnson's home by her daughter who was concerned that her mother was 'suffering' and needed to be seen. Upon arrival, her daughter escorted me to what was the dining room in the daughter's home that now was where Mrs. Johnson was in her hospital bed so she could be part of the daily routine of the family. Mrs. Johnson had a stroke leaving her left side paralyzed and now was in the later phase of the dying process, unable to eat and minimal communication. As I approached the bed, Mrs. Johnson was focused on an area at the top of the wall to her right side, pointing randomly at the area and speaking in words that were incomprehensible for her daughter and I to understand.

To demonstrate how to be with the dying, I approached the bed very quietly, reverently allowing Mrs. Johnson to continue to look away. Also, using all my senses paying attention to her daughter and expressing to her that her mother was not suffering. When Mrs. Johnson relaxed her right arm, I softly called her name and she looked in our direction, smiling and obviously recognizing her daughter. She was able to nod to questions about her current condition and where she was, indicating that she was able to return to the current dimension.

After a while, her daughter and I left the room while she rested and I explained that Mrs. Johnson was visiting a 'realm' that we were unable to understand from where we were and her mother was beginning her transition. Her attention to the area above the wall and her language was evidence enough that Mrs. Johnson's daughter could accept and be assured that her mother was not suffering.

Was this the Truth? How could I understand that this was really happening? As we become quiet, still and enter the 'grace' of the dying, information is given to share with the family that is comforting. As I entered the room, I had no idea what was 'really' going on with Mrs. Johnson, however the information about her transition was given and carefully shared with her daughter. It was not important that I was 'right' about the situation, all that was required was that the daughter could enter into this sacred space and be with her mother in her final hours. Mrs. Johnson died overnight hours after my visit.

345

Standing By & Standing Firm

I want to share a story with you from my work at the Veterans' hospital some years ago. We were near our end-of-life interdisciplinary team meeting when one of the inpatient nurses called me out of the meeting to let me know that our patient, who had recently transferred from SICU, had died and his son had been the one to find him.

We were expecting Mr. Thomas however were not told that he was on the floor and been transferred. The end-of-life and palliative care physician fellow accompanied me to the room to meet with Mr. Thomas, Jr., the patient's son. As we entered the room, I walked to the bed, glancing at the patient, and then I noticed a very husky, well-dressed gentleman who turned from the open window to face me across his father's bed. Before I could formulate what I might say, he began to express his anger as he moved forcefully toward me with the bed between us. He shared that he was a minister; he knew a lot about death and he knew about suffering. "I promised my father he would not suffer, and now he has. He died alone! I did not keep my promises to him," he shouted. Time stands still in many different experiences in one's life, and this was one such moment. It seemed like he would never stop shouting his anger in my direction, though it was only for a few minutes in reality.

When he finally stopped, I calmly said, "I will leave you with your father; let us know when you are ready for us to come back in." As I turned to walk out, the physician fellow was standing with her back against the door, hand on the knob, and tears were flowing down her face. This young physician was overwhelmed by the energy of the anger expressed. She would have been unlikely to formulate a response in the absence of a mystery-watcher's expertise. As we talked outside Mr. Thomas's room, she reflected on this emotionally draining situation and began to understand that the anger could only create a problem for her if she "took it on." She was still nervous that the son would blame our team for his father's "suffering."

After debriefing with the team, I left the nurse's station to begin the process of postmortem care with Mr. Thomas when Mr. Thomas, Jr. came out of the room. His face was soft, his eyes clear, and he walked directly toward me. We stopped and he looked deeply into my eyes, connecting at a spirit level, and I 'knew' that he was now at peace with the way his father had died. He apologized and thanked me for everything that was done for his father. I was surprised by the apology for his behavior and even more surprised when he asked for a hug.

In this moment, the power of connecting normalized his raw grief, and my ability to stand firm in the anger storm was the vehicle through which this healing came about. He would still need to reflect much more on the circumstances of his father's death, his own feeling of guilt, and ways he could help his family cope with this profound loss. However he had started his grief work moving closer to understanding the power of the mystery.

Accepting the Mystery

One of the hospice agencies I worked with had an in-patient floor in the adjacent hospital to our office. We received a call early during our team meeting that Mr. Brown was being transported to our hospice unit with pain and was in distress. I left the meeting to walk over to the unit to be sure the staff could get the orders and provide the treatment Mr. Brown would need.

As they brought Mr. Brown into the room, he was accompanied by his two daughters, both in the 35-45 year-old range, one was calm and supportive and the other was visibly distraught. In hospice we allow the family to be present, assist in the care, or self-select to wait outside. Both daughters elected to stay in the room as we moved Mr. Brown into the bed and began our assessment.

After we assessed Mr. Brown, I began telling the staff what we needed to do, get bloodwork, order medications, etc. Then, as I stood at the foot of the bed, like a bolt of lightning, I realized he was dying! This was hospice!! I told the staff to stop the orders and put a sign on the door to allow the family to be with Mr. Brown.

Both daughters came to his bedside on the right side and the distraught daughter stood behind her sister, softly crying. The hospice nurse and I allowed them to be with their father when I realized he stopped breathing. Both daughters realized it as well and their emotions increased with the recognition. After the appropriate amount of time. I quietly moved to the left side of the bed and began the assessment to pronounce Mr. Brown dead. I listened for his heart for over a minute and felt no pulse or any breathing. Then I nodded to the daughters that he was dead and the younger daughter began crying uncontrollably. I moved back to the foot of the bed to 'hold space' for the experience when I could not believe what I saw!

Mr. Brown, who was clinically dead, opened his eyes, smiled, turned his head toward his daughter who was crying and said "I Love YOU"! She stopped crying immediately. The nurse who was in the room looked at me and ran out of the room. Mr. Brown was clinically dead. And, yes, when I checked again, he was still clinically dead. However, this was one experience that confirmed how to accept the mystery.

Alzheimer & Other Concurrent Conditions

One thing I have noticed over the years is that with Alzheimer patients, when they get a death diagnosis, whatever other kinds of conditions they might have had, they disappear. I have met people diagnosed with heart issues, and dying because of these heart issues and whose Alzheimer condition got really bad, their heart condition got better. It could be that at the time the stress is gone. Once you get rid of the emotion, the stress is gone.

This was also this gentleman who had been found to have a big tumor on his neck before he developed Alzheimer, a tumor that, by all intent and purposes, should be cutting down his breathing and blood supply, but he was doing just fine. The tumor continued growing, but this guy was doing just fine, still eating and sleeping, not in pain. The stress was gone, and so was the emotion and the pain.

Mrs. Charity

Mrs. Charity was a 93 year old 'matriarch' living in a memory care unit. She was admitted into our hospice agency with the diagnosis of Alzheimer's Disease some 2 years prior to my employment and was not showing any decline. When it becomes time to continue her care and 'keep her in hospice', the payor source was indicating that we needed to discharge her because she was not worse. This was the 'chicken and the egg' metaphor for me. Was Mrs. Charity not getting worse because we were involved in her care or was she just not getting worse? After long discussions in our interdisciplinary team meeting, we reviewed her past history charts and found that she had been diagnosed with heart disease, high blood pressure and breast cancer in the past. Currently she was 'stable' and none of those were causing her any problem, however when I contacted her cancer physician, we learned she did not receive the 'traditional' treatment for cancer because she had dementia, which they and the family believed this would cause her to decline much faster. So, with her cancer physician agreeing, we changed her diagnosis to breast cancer with dementia and she was able to remain in our care.

Mrs. Charity lived 6 more months, stopped eating and slowly declined eventually dying in the 'home' that was very familiar to her with her staff 'family' and her biological family with her.

Of note here, one very important point is often overlooked by medical staff (hospice, etc.) when someone is ill or dies: The institutional staff, especially the ones caring every day for the mentally declining people are often overlooked and the biological families come in and are now the 'family'. The staff should be included in the rituals at death along with the biological family since they have been the primary caregivers that the dying person has seen every day. They grieve as well and need the support of the counseling staff and other family members.

Similar Case of Two Families

Mrs. Fleming was in her late 70's, family matriarch had cancer that did not allow her to swallow. The family wanted her to have artificial nutrition so she could live longer. So they had a PEG tube placed in her stomach and we had to teach the family how to use the tube, what to look for, and how to take care of her. They took her home and we delivered all the equipment such as the hospital bed, the bedside commode, suction machine, etc. We would go periodically and make sure everything was ok because she had awful problems. It was just like with a baby, when fed with artificial food, you need to find something their system can use. When you put in a stomach PEG tube, you have to figure out what is compatible with their system.

Among other problems, Mrs. Fleming had diarrhea because the food does not flow through the stomach and the esophagus like it would normally. It goes straight into the intestines and it goes straight down. Sometimes it goes into the duodenum which is just past the stomach. As a consequence, they have all kinds of problems with digestion. They have constant gas, gargling, and diarrhea. And then the diarrhea causes the breakdown on the bottom, so you end up with all these issues such as yeast infection, and all kinds of stuff goes wrong. It was a battle taking care of this lady at home. The worst part was that she did not have a caregiver that was consistent. The family kept taking turns so we were constantly going in and retraining and helping. It was very difficult.

Around the same time, we admitted another woman into hospice also in her 70s, Mrs. Parker, whose husband and son wanted to take her home. They lived in a rural area, she was taken home and was not able to swallow, nor eat nor drink either. She had a brain aneurysm (bleeding in the brain) and was pretty much bed bound. Her family said they did not want artificial feeding because they felt it was not what she had wanted.

Her hospital bed was in the living room looking out the window at her bird feeders. For a while she was unconscious, but after a while she woke up still unable to get out of bed. She could not talk, but she could let her family know what she needed. We taught her family how to take care of her. They took excellent care of this matriarch. They spent time with her, and kept her bird feeders full as she really enjoyed the birds.

Both of these ladies lived 8 weeks from the moment they were admitted into hospice. When you artificially feed somebody it is like you 'unscrew their heart, you pour water in and screw it back on'. Artificial feeding bypasses the normal system and it does not satisfy hunger. Chewing and swallowing produces satiety; artificial feeding never satisfies.

Mrs. Flemming, who was artificially fed was 'drowning' because she could not manage all the feeding. Her body was shutting down, however she was still being fed. Often at the end of their life, the fluid accumulates in the lungs and the 'death rattle' occurs leaving a difficult memory for the family.

Mrs. Parker's experience was very different. Her body slowly shut down. Since she was dying, she did not require food or fluid. The increased pressure in her brain went down because she was not being 'artificially fed'. She was able to interact with her family and watch her birds feeding.

Hospice personnel do not have a lot of choice about the feeding method because often when we admitted the patients, the decision had already been made.

FEAR
FALSE EVIDENCE APPEARING REAL

'Forget Everything And Run'
or
'Face Everything And Rise'

Spirit Leaving Through Her Head

As a new hospice nurse, many times we would do what we call joined visits and either visit with the social worker or the chaplain. On this day with the chaplain we went to see Mrs. Cline, who had been in hospice for a while. The chaplain knew her really well and he would go and spend time with her, read scripture, and play the piano (he sang beautifully). He would play some of her favorite hymns, as in this particular visit. While he played in the living room, I was in the bedroom helping her husband clean her up. As it usually happens, the husband was anxious so he was busy cleaning up the room, not paying much attention to what I was doing.

I was standing on her left side, by the bed and I had my left hand just laying on top of her head, my right hand was on her right arm and I was watching her husband busy himself. I felt a sensation in my left hand like she was gritting her teeth. A lot of time, when someone has a seizure, they may clinch their teeth as though 'gritting their teeth'. So I looked down at her and her face was very peaceful, and I realized she had changed. 'What is going on?'

I could feel the opening in the palm of my hand where the 'foramen ovale' is located like the soft spot of the baby's head. All of a sudden, I felt the bones at the top of her head shift, and it felt like a numbness, and an energy. It was really fast, but I knew instantly what was happening. The energy went through my hand, I felt her spirit come out of her body, go across my arm, it went down my shoulder, through the other arm and it went to the living room and into the chaplain who was playing the hymns. I think he was playing 'Amazing Grace'. And all of a sudden, he was just banging it loud on the piano. It was really loud. I called the husband over where I was and told him I thought the wife was gone. He was able to hold her hand and give her a kiss before she took her last breath.

The Chaplain and I did everything you have to do when death occurs. I made calls to the funeral home and the physician. We waited for the body to be removed and made sure her husband was comfortable before we left.

On the way back to the office, I asked the Chaplain, "Why were you playing that song so loud?" He said, "that was her." He said, "I was ready to quit and she wanted me to keep playing, I couldn't quit".

She passed through me and into him. I felt it, he felt it, we knew it was her.

Some People Choose Dying Alone

A hospice colleague asked me to go with her to the adjoining hospital to visit her grandmother, Nanna Jones, who had been 'dying' for a week and seemed to be unable to transition. I knew my colleague was very aware of energies and often saw 'angelic' beings in the rooms of some of our clients we visited, however because it was her Nanna, she was unable to 'see' the reason she could not transition.

As we arrived in the darkened hospital room at the end of the hall reserved for dying patients, the lights were dimmed, and the room was filled with family. I am sure there were lots of 'ancestors' present as well, since I am uncomfortable in a crowded room, I felt like I could not breathe. The conversations were loud with several people unaware that I had come into the room.

Nanna was lying quietly, unresponsive to presence or to touch or soft whispers. As I entered her energetic space I felt welcomed and a warmness from the area of her bed. Most of the family were sitting around or standing near the walls and windows and many unaware of what was going on at the bedside.

After a few minutes it became very clear that Nanna could not die with all these people in the room. Wow!! This is a family's culture was to 'be there' in Love for the dying so 'how could I share this with this family?' Was I right to think this?

I invited my 'friend' to go with me into the hall outside the room. When we were out of earshot of the others, I shared my impression with her. She began to smile and said "OF COURSE! Nanna loves her quiet time!" The rest of the story you can guess. I left the hospital and she returned to the room to share her feelings with those in the room. They all agreed and paid their regards to Nanna as they left the room. My friend was the last to leave and shared with me later that when they returned sometime later, Nanna had transitioned 'Peacefully', alone as she wished.

This story has many insights or lessons. First, trust your instincts or intuition and share that. The others can accept or reject your ideas, however you are true to what you believe. Second, culturally our stereotypical ideas can get in the way of the intuition which in this case, my determination that this culture had certain beliefs and this was not the case. Lastly, my friend had gifts with others however when it came to her Nanna, she was 'too close' to see what her Nanna needed. We still have a LOT to learn.

Mrs. Lucy

Mrs. Lucy was an elderly lady who lived in the country with her husband who was extremely hard of hearing, almost deaf. She had an end-of-life diagnosis of colon cancer. She was in quite a bit of pain, so one of our nurses went out there to assess her and figured out that it would be better if she had a pump that gave her medicine all the time. Mrs. Lucy had a little bit of dementia, so it was difficult at first to get her to carry the pump around to keep from discontinuing the medication going to the needle in her subcutaneous tissue (Sub-Q). We got called a couple of times about her pulling the needle out, and we had to go back and put it in, no matter what time of the day or night to keep her comfortable.

On this particular day, we got the call that she had pulled it out again and when we got there, Mrs. Lucy apologized and apologized. We found that she had gotten up to go to the bathroom and she left the pump on the couch and picked up her house shoe instead of the pump. She thought the house shoe was her pump, so when she went to the bathroom, it pulled out and the pump was still sitting on the couch. The nurse had to just laugh because Mrs. Lucy thought she was doing it right and carrying her pump with her.

Stories of ALS

There is a sense of Grace when someone dies and obviously there is a Divine Being. There is a big umbrella of Grace that is over everyone involved in the transition at death. It can be one of the most peaceful, wonderful situations when somebody is allowed to go through the death process and not 'treated to death'.

Between 2012-15 as part of the VA system, we cared for many veterans with ALS. One of the directors of the VA said investigating many causes revealed the only common denominator was boot camp. At first it was soldiers in the Gulf war, however statistics revealed vetcrans were ten times more likely to develop ALS than the general public. The stress of boot camp molded soldiers to a 'yes' person who would do anything for the mission, taking power away from them.

After years of study by the Veteran's Affairs revealed different kinds of ALS. Previously while working in hospice, ALS was diagnosed by loss of motor control, inability to walk then loss of use of their hands, difficulty breathing and death. These patients often had several months to years to decide about having feeding tube or respiratory support measures taken and could make decisions that were in line with their beliefs.

Many of the Veterans in our care presented to the hospital with respiratory failure. They couldn't breathe! The decision to provide respiratory support was made in the emergency room and stabilized in the intensive care units and they could never discontinue this support. They could still move and walk but they just could not talk or breathe without a ventilator machine.

Mr. Guthrey

Mr. Guthrey was one such veteran, who had very limited use of his hands and had lost mobility everywhere in his body. His wife was the primary health caregiver, and they had no children. She was with him all the time 24/7 as he was dependent on his BiPap machine which he wore a mask that assisted with his breathing. They were delightful and he had made the decision he did not want a trache tube, nor a feeding tube. He had decided that when he could not eat anymore, he was done. Many clients often wait for the family to make the decision, however Mr. Guthrey was very sure about his decisions and had shared and documented those wishes.

His wife called frantic one day because his machine stopped working. It took about an hour to reach their home which was over 50 miles from the VA. Mrs. Guthrey met me at the door and was visibly upset recounting that the breathing machine he depended on had stopped working and he could not breathe. She had a backup machine however she could not remember where it was.

He was unable to breathe as his wife was squeezing the balloon on his mask so he could get some air keeping her from finding the replacement. Finally, she went to look for it and the husband stayed without air for about 4 minutes. His wife was so upset because she thought she was 'going to kill him'. By the time I arrived, he was breathing easily and resting, with no worsting of his condition while Mrs. Guthrey was in need of a calm presence. This was a great lesson to have the backup ready and they scheduled a meeting with very close friends to be sure Mrs. Guthrey was supported.

Mr. Guthrey eventually declined and could not swallow anymore so his wife honored his wishes not to do anything else. He died peacefully in the middle of the night.

Meet Tom

The social worker and I visited Tom, who the VA had paid for his house to be outfitted for a disability because he was a veteran. He had been in the ICU for over a month with 'respiratory failure' and was sent home on a ventilator and was diagnosed with ALS. He could live without the ventilator for a very short time when we first met him, however he could not talk because he had a tracheostomy tube in his neck. He also had use of his legs however his arms were paralyzed and he could barely breathe on his own.

As his condition worsened, he required the ventilator connected most of the time. If he got hungry, he could not call out, could not use his hands, however he could still walk around. He would get out of bed, and walk into the kitchen where wife was and he would just bump into her, and she would know he needed something; and she had to figure out what he needed.

He was in hospice also and he lived for probably six or eight months. He slowly declined requiring more time on his ventilator and not being able to walk only because he could not breathe. Tom was a very interesting person and he was really funny. His wife knew how to take care of him and it was fascinating to watch the dynamics between the two of them.

Eventually, he progressed to being bed-bound, unable to communicate using his electronic equipment provided by the VA and he died at home.

Mr. Melton

Mr. Melton, who also had ALS, had suffered from heart problems for a while. He was still able to get around a little bit slowly and he lived with his wife who was his caregiver. Mr. Melton would use oxygen at night, but most of the time he was able to breathe and swallow on his own.

Mrs. Melton had a son who moved in with them to help his mother care for Mr. Melton. Her son was dependent to a machine all the time that helped his failing heart beat and he was waiting on a heart transplant.

One night, Mrs. Melton woke up to realize she could not hear her son's machine. It had stopped working and he had died. He was there to help her care for Mr. Melton and now he had died first. This complex grief was too much for Mrs. Melton and she could not care for Mr. Melton anymore so, he was taken to a facility where he died in just a few days.

Mr. Flynn

Mr. Flynn was a veteran who had been in hospice for over a year when I met him. He was living at home in the country with loving his wife and kids who were all very involved in caring for him. He was totally bed bound, had a feeding tube and was completely dependent on a ventilator for about two years. All he could do was blink his eyes which Mrs. Flynn understood. She was knowledgeable about the situation and how to care for him, feeding through a tube, manage his breathing machine and turn him every two hours.

On a visit with the social worker, the wife told us Mr. Flynn was ready to go. The family had had a big reunion the previous weekend and asked him yes or no questions. He told them he did not want to live like this anymore; he was done. He had developed a respiratory infection and he had taken so many antibiotics in the last two years that this time the medicine was not working. With the home hospice team involved, a date was set to take him off of the ventilator. Our team consisted of our physician, the chaplain and a social worker from the VA. The hospice team provided nursing with the medication that we would need to keep him calm before he could comfortably come off the ventilator. We had to make sure that he could blink because that was the only thing that he could do to let us know how he was feeling.

His wife knew him so well that, although he had his eyes closed, she could tell the amount of medicine the hospice staff had given him was not enough. He had a large amount of the calming medicine and Mrs. Flynn was confident he was ready for to remove the ventilator. I asked the wife if she wanted to do it and she said: "Oh, I plan to!" She wanted to be the one to take the breathing tube off so she took it off just to see how he would react and he began gasping for air. We realized the wife was right and she immediately put the ventilator back on. After a little more medicine and after a few more minutes the wife then told us he

was ready now. After a few minutes of silence, the wife got up and turned the switch off. After about 5 minutes, his heart stopped.

This couple had been communicating for months through his eye movement and just by looking at him with his eyes closed, Mrs. Flynn could tell if her husband was awake or not. The family was appropriately grieving however most of the grieving had occurred over the many years he had been completely dependent. The hospice team cared for the body and we all felt blessed by Grace to have been part of this amazing transition.

Mom's Favorite Color

Damn this rain. I'm sick of it. Sick of putting on a happy face and smiling at all the residents.

Everyday . . .same conversation with each of them. "Good morning Mrs Sonjania, How are you today?"

"Oh my heart is going to quit any day unless my sciatica takes me first."

I gotta get to the store today . . . Soup sounds like a good idea for dinner tonight. Mrs. Glenn's passing was a shock. I thought she was feeling better.

How better is 'better' tho when you're 89.

At least she went fast . . . And her daughter was so good to her.

How lucky was it that I was home when Mom stroked out. I knew she was leaving . . .

Wow! She's been gone ten years. I can't believe it. Ten Years!

Who knew I would miss her more and more instead of less and less.

I'm such a wimp. I don't know why I get choked up over her ten years later.

. . .What was her favorite Color

God . . . I don't even know what her favorite color was.

What kind of daughter am I? Jeez. I suck!

. . . Wonder what Mrs. Glenn's favorite color was? Wonder if her daughter knows? Tomorrow I'm asking her.

And I'm going to ask all my clients and write it down. Yea . . .   Then their families will know . . .

Potato soup.

That's what I'm fixing tonight.   Least I do know that was Mom's favorite soup.

"Hi babe . . . Yes, I'm almost at the store.   How does potato soup sound for dinner?"

". . . OK, that's settled then. See you in a bit, and by the way . . . Is your favorite color still orange?"

Sylvia DeVoss aka. Peacewogs

Final Thoughts

My dream for this book is to have an opportunity to share art and stories of the brave souls and their families in the process of dying. Since I learned that 100% of us will die, I believe that welcoming death as a part of our life needs to be shared. I would love for this book to be part of 'coffee-table' reading to share without fear of death.

Many of the photos in this book are computer digitalized and others were taken at various places with other cameras. Sylvia is a master with the digital computer photos so please enjoy and feel what they bring up in your energy field. Many of the photos have been taken along my journey.

This fulfills part of my purpose in this lifetime to be able to share with you the beauty of artistic photography with the beauty of the stories shared by the dying.

You matter because you are you. You matter until the last moment of your life, and we will do all we can, not only to help you die peacefully, but also to live until you die.

-Dame Cicely Saunders

Cover art by Sylvia DeVoss

First Printing: 2023

ISBN: 979-8-8689-1471-3
Library of Congress Control Number: 2023920342

SUPPOSE, LLC
Richmond, VA 23225

www.supposellc.com

Acknowledgments

Creator had an amazing sense-of-humor when we created this life for me. Spiritual experiences have been part of my life and has lead me to appreciate those who have gone before and shared their stories. Thank YOU.

For the Johanna Giraldo for her encouragement in completing this book by assisting with transcribing and editing the text.

Sylvia DeVoss provided much of the art in this book and assisted with the positioning and editing for your enjoyment. You can connect with Sylvia at www.sylviadevoss.com about her artwork. Thanks from Sylvia to Jackie for the "Phoenix Rising" photo on the next page.

Spiritual Gifts Keep Giving! When you Pay ATTENTION!

Dedication

What a Journey! To those who have supported my life and others who sought to change me.

I have learned so much and please know that I am grateful for each and every one.

A special dedication to all those from my birth, through religious indoctrination, into the several life-partnerships bearing one child, and finally in the spiritual aspect of working with the dying. Include your names if you know you influenced me.

For Diane who has witnessed and experienced the transition and been an amazing spirit both working with the dying and in our lives together.

I Love YOU!

They told her she could fly..
so she tried and tried
and tried and tried
and try try tried
and kept tryin
and then
she died

46

Bypass the Gurus.. Learn from the Children.. Believe in your SELF.

www.ingramcontent.com/pod-product-compliance
Lightning Source LLC
Chambersburg PA
CBHW041032120726
48005CB00004B/787